Keeping A Pet
TORTOISE

Keeping A Pet
TORTOISE

How to set up home for a new tortoise and keep it in the best of health and condition

ANDREW HIGHFIELD AND NADINE HIGHFIELD

Interpet Publishing

Published by Interpet Publishing,
Vincent Lane, Dorking,
Surrey RH4 3YX,
England

Reprinted 2010, 2011, 2012,
2013, 2014

ISBN 978-1-84286-213-1

Credits

Editor: Philip de Ste. Croix
Designer: Phil Clucas MSIAD
Diagram artwork: Martin Reed
Production management: Consortium,
    Poslingford, Suffolk
Print production: 1010 Printing
    International Ltd
Printed and bound in China

The recommendations in this
book are given without any
guarantees on the part of the
author and publisher. If in
doubt, seek the advice of a
vet or pet-care specialist.

The Authors

Andy C. Highfield has worked with tortoises and turtles for almost 30 years and co-founded the Tortoise Trust with the late Jill Martin in 1984. He subsequently published the highly influential *Keeping & Breeding Tortoises in Captivity* in 1990, and went on to write the *Tortoise Trust Guide to Tortoises and Turtles* in 1994, and the *Practical Encyclopaedia of Keeping and Breeding Tortoises and Freshwater Turtles* in 1996. He has published numerous scientific papers, has contributed to most of the major reptile-keeping magazines both as author and photographer, has lectured all over the world on tortoise conservation and captive management, acted as consultant on numerous media projects and developed the world's first online course in chelonian husbandry. He continues to act as director of the Tortoise Trust, and is also chairman of the Jill Martin Fund for Tortoise Welfare and Conservation. He is widely acknowledged as one of the world's foremost authorities on the conservation and captive propagation of tortoises and turtles.

Nadine Highfield was raised around turtles in New Jersey and Rhode Island, and this led to her developing a lifelong interest in their conservation, rescue and rehabilitation. She has published many articles on their care, and currently is in charge of rehabilitating critically ill rescues at the Tortoise Trust in the UK. She has also acted as a technical consultant and editor on various reference texts, and has advised major companies on the conservation and welfare impacts of tortoise and turtle imagery in television advertising and media campaigns. She is especially interested in educating young people about responsible pet care and welfare issues. She is also a skilled natural history photographer.

Contents

Introduction

Tortoises have always been extremely popular pets, but they have never been easy pets to look after. Although they have a popular reputation as relatively easy and undemanding, quite the opposite is true. In general terms, all reptile pets have very precise environmental and dietary requirements. Tortoises are no exception.

Tortoises occur around the world in a very wide range of different habitats, from humid rain forests to arid deserts, and in regions that experience harsh winters to those that have no winter season at all. In each case, they have developed very special strategies and behaviours in response to these environments. These factors must be considered carefully when deciding which species to keep. The very different environmental and nutritional needs of the various species means that you cannot rely on too many generalities when considering tortoises. It is absolutely critical to consider each individual species carefully in its own right.

> Tortoises occur around the world in a very wide range of different habitats, they have developed very special strategies and behaviours in response to their environments.

Do your homework

The mortality rate among tortoises purchased as pets is extremely high. Most of these deaths are entirely avoidable if you do adequate research in advance, and make sure you fully understand what you are getting into. On no account should you buy a tortoise on impulse without consulting reliable information on its needs beforehand. It is also best to cross-check any information you are given with at least one other reliable source. There is, unfortunately, a lot of very poor and even dangerous information out there, especially in out-of-date books and on the Internet.

This book is by no means an exhaustive list of all the possible species that you might encounter, but it does cover the species most often seen in pet stores. There are many other species, some of which have strict legal prohibitions upon sale and ownership. In all cases, you should establish if there are any legal restrictions in force in respect of the species you are interested in. Even many common species, such as Mediterranean *Testudo* species, are now subject to various regulations under the CITES (Convention on International Trade in Endangered Species) treaty, and may therefore require possession of special permits in order to sell or

transport them. Many species throughout the world are also protected by local wildlife legislation in addition to restrictions under CITES and any form of possession, whether it involves taking from the wild or even captive breeding, may be subject to strict limits or an outright ban.

Remember that cute little juveniles may grow into huge adults.

Above *It is a misconception that tortoises are easy pets to keep. In fact, each species demands a particular regime of care that responsible owners should understand before acquiring one.*

Left *Don't assume that you can simply leave a pet tortoise to fend for itself in the garden. It needs much more care than that.*

Below *Wild-caught tortoises are often kept in very poor conditions and such trade is also highly illegal.*

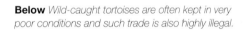

General guidelines

When thinking about keeping a tortoise,
there are a great many issues to consider
at the very outset. These include:

Size and space requirements

Tortoises, despite what you may hear
elsewhere, are not suitable for keeping in a
vivarium environment on a permanent basis.
No tortoise can be kept successfully and
humanely in a glass tank. Even small
species need a lot more space than
you might initially think. In addition, some
species, especially leopard *(Geochelone
pardalis)* and African spurred *(Geochelone
sulcata)* tortoises are capable of reaching
truly massive sizes as adults. Do you really

Above *This picture of a leopard tortoise walking in
its natural environment in South Africa reveals just
how large an adult of this type can grow.*

want to end up with a pet that is so large
that you cannot even pick it up? You would
be surprised at just how many people make
the mistake of buying a 'cute little tortoise'
without realising that within just a few years
it will turn into a 20kg (50lb) giant.

Indoor and outdoor
housing needs

All species require access to secure and
safe indoor and outdoor facilities. If you live
in a cooler climate, you will have to provide
appropriate lighting and heating facilities for
several months a year. Outdoor pens must
not be only be escape-proof, but also fully
secured against potential predators getting
in. We will discuss detailed housing
requirements later in this book.

Safety and hygiene

You should not under any circumstances
mix different species or animals from different
geographical origins, as not only do they
often have entirely incompatible nutritional
and environmental requirements, but their
behaviour patterns are often incompatible
as well. Stress and serious injuries will result
from allowing contact between different
species. In addition, many species carry
disease-causing organisms that other
species have little or no resistance to, so
mixing them (or even allowing brief contact or
cross-contamination to occur) can result in ill-
health and even the death of the susceptible
animal. The risk to human health is low, but
it does exist. All reptiles should be handled
with due care and attention to maintaining
adequate hygiene. No contact between
tortoises and human food preparation areas
should ever be allowed, and your hands
should be washed thoroughly with an
antibacterial soap after handling any tortoise.
It is just as important to wash your hands in
between handling different species. This is
an extremely important part of tortoise
husbandry, and by taking such precautions

you will greatly reduce the risk of disease and avoid costly veterinary treatment.

Choose a captive-bred animal

Unless you have decided to adopt a turtle or tortoise from a rescue organisation, always choose genuine captive-bred animals over wild-caught specimens. Because of the stress of collection, long-distance shipping, improper handling and inadequate care, turtles and tortoises that are wild-caught are far more prone to develop illnesses. They may have also come into contact with other species in the pet trade that could have had any number of contagious diseases. Be aware that a tortoise may appear perfectly healthy, and yet it may already be infected with a serious illness or a high level of parasitic infection that will soon require veterinary treatment.

This may seem like a daunting list of factors to consider, and in some ways it is. However, all of these things are manageable given adequate planning and preparation. Keeping tortoises as pets, however, is not something to be undertaken lightly. In the following sections we will examine each of these areas in detail, and we will establish some reliable ground rules to ensure that both you and your new tortoise get off to the best possible start together.

Left *Mixing different species can result in serious injuries, such as this shell damage.*

Below *Always choose a captive-bred animal over a wild-caught one. It is much more likely to be healthy and free of parasites.*

Mediterranean and Russian tortoises

In this section we will look at the commonly kept Mediterranean tortoises and the Russian tortoise, both members of the genus *Testudo*. In terms of care, Russian tortoises and Mediterranean tortoises are very similar indeed. Most (but not all) members of this genus hibernate over winter.

Mediterranean tortoises

This group includes *Testudo graeca* (the so-called 'Greek' or spur-thighed tortoise), *Testudo hermanni* (Hermann's tortoise) and *Testudo marginata* (the marginated tortoise). This is a very complex group, comprising a large number of different geographical forms, subspecies, and disputed species. Broadly speaking, the *Testudo graeca* group is the most challenging of all, and there are major differences between animals from different geographical areas that pose special problems to those who describe and classify species (taxonomists). There are at least two, and possibly as many as four, different types within the *Testudo hermanni* complex, and even the status of *Testudo marginata* has been questioned. The spur-thighed tortoises can be divided into two main groups based upon geographical origin:

The North African complex

Spur-thighed tortoises occur from the south of Morocco, through Algeria, Tunisia and Libya. They also occur in the south of Spain and on some of the Spanish islands. There are considerable differences evident between animals from all of these locations. In some parts of this large and diverse range, tortoises hibernate over winter, in other places they aestivate (lie dormant) during the heat of summer. In some localities, both hibernation and aestivation occurs.

The Asiatic and Middle Eastern complex

This particular complex within the spur-thighed group occurs throughout Turkey, in areas bordering the Black Sea, and in various locations throughout the Middle East. The spur-thighed tortoises of Turkish origin have been designated as *Testudo ibera*. Their general behaviour in the wild is very similar to that of the North African *Testudo graeca*, but in terms of their behaviour with other tortoises there are major differences. For example, they are typically far more aggressive and bite and 'ram' each other much more so than their North African relatives. This is important when keeping these animals in captivity, as serious injuries can result if tortoises with incompatible behaviours are allowed to mix.

continued

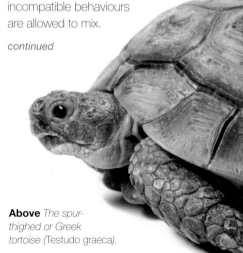

Above *The spur-thighed or Greek tortoise (*Testudo graeca*).*

Left *A Libyan origin Mediterranean tortoise,* Testudo graeca cyrenaica.

Below right *The popular Hermann's tortoise,* Testudo hermanni.

Above *Typical habitat in Turkey in which* Testudo ibera *is found.*

Below *In captivity,* Testudo graeca *requires a spacious, dry, well-drained pen. Fresh water should be available at all times.*

Mediterranean and Russian tortoises

The Horsfield's or Russian tortoise (Testudo horsfieldii)

This tortoise is not a Mediterranean dweller; it occurs in the steppes and mountainous regions of Central Asia, including Pakistan, Afghanistan and the former Soviet Asian republics. In the wild, this tortoise has a very short period of activity – just a few months – and the rest of the time it is either hibernating to avoid the extreme cold or aestivating to avoid extreme heat. It is a relatively easy species to keep in captivity. The main captive requirements are for a very dry, low humidity substrate, and the ability to create scrapes and burrows. If maintained in conditions that are cold, damp or high in humidity, Russian tortoises will quickly succumb to potentially fatal respiratory, skin and shell infections. Like other members of the genus *Testudo*, it is a herbivore that requires a carefully balanced diet of flowers and fresh green vegetation. Animal protein should **never** be offered. This species can (and should) be hibernated in captivity, provided the animals are well established and healthy.

Ideal care conditions

In terms of general captive husbandry, however, all of these tortoises require broadly similar care. They are all herbivorous, and require a low protein, high fibre, calcium-rich diet based on leaves and flowers. They all require relatively dry, well-drained substrates and warm conditions, with adequate facilities for basking. They should also be provided with fresh drinking water at all times. In most cases, these tortoises hibernate naturally in the wild and can do so in captivity. However, as mentioned earlier, some geographic forms from certain areas do not hibernate in the wild and subjecting these to hibernation in captivity can be dangerous. It is, therefore, very important to establish precisely which form you actually have. It is beyond the scope of this particular book to describe all of the possibilities and their care requirements in sufficient detail. Specialist tortoise societies are the best source of further advice on this subject.

> The main captive requirements are for a very dry, low humidity substrate, and the ability to create scrapes and burrows.

Left *This Russian tortoise is pictured in a hemp-based substrate. Hemp is popular for use in indoor terrariums and also for overnight bedding. However, it contains very hard, sharp splinters that pose an unacceptable danger to tortoises. They may cause penetrative injuries or be ingested which can lead to death. We do not recommend its use for tortoise keeping.*

Below *The Egyptian tortoise, Testudo kleinmanni, requires a dry and sandy habitat.*

Below left *A male Russian tortoise. In captivity, it is essential to provide a very secure pen as these tortoises are exceptionally agile and persistent escapers, capable of burrowing underground.*

Below Testudo horsfieldii.

Below *The Horsfield's, or Russian, tortoise is frequently kept as a pet.*

Tropical tortoises from dry habitats

Tropical tortoises occur in a wide range of sizes, and are found in an equally wide range of habitats, from dry grasslands, to deserts, to true tropical rainforests. None of these species hibernates, a factor that should be carefully considered, as they will require adequate heat and light 365 days a year.

Above *The leopard tortoise is an attractively marked animal which favours semi-arid habitats.*

Leopard tortoises

Leopard tortoises *(Geochelone pardalis)* are found throughout southern Africa, where they occur in grassy, scrubby habitats. Although often sold as pets when young, it is vitally important to realise that as adults this species reaches a very large size indeed. Large examples may be 60cm (over 2ft) long and weigh over 35kg (about 80lb).

This species does not hibernate, so it will require warm accommodation all year round, and feeding can also prove difficult during periods when they cannot go outside due to unsuitable weather conditions. This is not a species to take on without careful

consideration, as the commitment and cost involved is very substantial indeed. In captivity, this species requires a lot of space, with warm, dry shelter available at all times, and daily access to an outdoor grazing area.

Leopard tortoises require a substantial amount of exercise and in no way should ever be regarded as a vivarium or indoor animal. Leopard tortoises are animals of the great African savannahs, and if deprived of grass and sufficient exercise soon develop a variety of health problems. Damp and cold are a serious problem for this species. Warm, dry conditions (with easy access to soaking and drinking water) are vital. Most keepers of leopard tortoises find that they need a combination of outdoor pens and large, heated, well insulated sheds or other buildings to provide indoor accommodation during cool weather. Leopard tortoises are very attractive animals, but do be sure that you fully appreciate just how much hard work (and expense) is involved before you decide to keep one.

African spurred tortoises

This extremely large tortoise must not be confused with the Mediterranean spur-thighed tortoise, which is not only very much smaller, but also has very different dietary and environmental needs. Unfortunately, many dealers confuse the two by incorrectly calling the African spurred tortoise the African spur-thighed tortoise. The correct name is African spurred tortoise, or *Geochelone sulcata*. It may also be referred to as the 'Sulcata tortoise'. The comments made regarding leopard tortoises also apply to the African spurred tortoise, but even more so! This is one of the world's largest tortoises, and they can attain carapace lengths of 83cm (over 2.5ft) and a maximum recorded weight of 105kg (about 240lb). continued

Above *Desert and arid habitat species generally have thick, overlapping scales on their legs.*

Below left *Typical dry habitat in the Western Cape region of South Africa.* **Below** *African spurred tortoises are among the largest tortoises in the world.*

Tropical tortoises from dry habitats

African spurred tortoises require a very large outdoor grazing area in a hot, dry climate. If you cannot provide this on a permanent basis, do not take this species on as a pet. Rescue centres around the world are overrun with specimens purchased by people who failed to appreciate just how difficult they are to keep. Not only are their space demands considerable, they also excavate giant burrows and can dig under fences and walls. Otherwise, conditions required are more or less identical to those demanded by the smaller, though still fairly large, leopard tortoise. Their diet is also similar to leopard tortoises in that a very high percentage of it needs to be high fibre mixed grasses. They do not hibernate. Two males should not be kept together as they can prove highly aggressive and can inflict serious damage on each other.

Indian star tortoises

This very attractively marked tortoise (*Geochelone elegans*) occurs in semi-arid, thorny and grassland habitats in Asia. As with all tropical-origin tortoises this species does not hibernate, and it will require spacious, warm accommodation all year round. Access to natural sunlight must be provided as often as possible, but take care not to allow the animal to overheat. Shade is equally essential, especially in hot climates. As with leopard tortoises, Indian star tortoises enjoy basking and require a bright, dry, warm environment if they are to thrive. If kept indoors, an oral vitamin D3 supplement must be given. Alternatively, use high output UV-B full spectrum lamps and change them regularly (see pages 44-45).

The Indian star tortoise is a strict herbivore. In captivity, it is a common error to

Above *The shell of the Indian star tortoise is designed to camouflage it by breaking up its body outline in the dry, grassy environment of the Indian subcontinent which is its natural habitat.*

feed too much soft, high-water-content food, such as lettuce, tomatoes and fruit. Instead, this tortoise requires a coarse, high fibre diet based around mixed grasses. Feeding excessive quantities of fruit frequently leads to severe gastric upsets. Star tortoises will graze happily on lawn grass and this seems to prevent most such problems at source. Meat products should **never** be given to star tortoises, nor should high protein vegetables, such as beans or peas, feature regularly in the diet. This leads to excessive growth,

poor bone formation, dangerously high blood-urea levels, bladder 'stones' and liver problems. Their demand for calcium and mineral trace elements is high so use of a supplement is critical.

Star tortoises like to drink and soak in shallow water, so always ensure that a clean bathing and drinking tray is provided. Do not mix with other species, as star tortoises are highly susceptible to catching diseases from other tortoises, even if those tortoises appear healthy themselves.

The head and front legs can be withdrawn into the shell as a method of self-defence.

Above *Typical habitat of the desert tortoise in North America.*

Left *The Indian star tortoise occurs in semi-arid, thorny and grassland habitats where it grazes extensively upon mixed grasses. Star tortoises can possess a shell with naturally raised scutes. This feature is highly variable – both smooth and quite bumpy specimens exist in the same populations.*

Tropical tortoises from humid habitats

Redfoot tortoises

The redfoot tortoise *(Geochelone carbonaria)* is perhaps the most common of all the South American tropical tortoises. Redfoot tortoises inhabit grassland savannah and forest habitats throughout South

America. This species does not hibernate. It also requires consistently warm temperatures in the 22-28°C range (72-83°F) both day and night. Humidity is also important to redfoot tortoises, and is especially critical to juveniles and hatchlings, which will become ill if kept too dry. A large soaking tray is essential, as redfoot tortoises greatly enjoy taking baths in lukewarm water on a daily basis.

Redfoot tortoises have an eclectic and varied diet. They are one of the few terrestrial tortoise species that is omnivorous. Their diet is based around 95 per cent flowers, green leaves and fruits with around 5 per cent

animal protein content. The yellowfoot tortoise *(Geochelone denticulata)* has essentially identical care requirements, with a preference for somewhat higher levels of ambient humidity. Adult redfoot tortoises are quite substantial animals, and like leopard tortoises, require a good deal of space. Provision of adequate levels of humidity in indoor and outdoor enclosures can prove difficult.

Hingeback tortoises

These *Kinixys* species take their common name from the fact that they are the only tortoise with a movable hinge on the rear of the shell that they use as a defence mechanism to protect their soft, fleshy parts from attack by predators. They are naturally found in the tropical regions of central Africa. All species of hingeback tortoises require constantly warm surroundings. Bell's hinged tortoise *(K. belliana)* can tolerate drier

Above *The redfoot is named on account of the bright red scales which adorn its legs in profusion.*

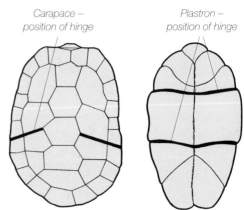

Carapace – position of hinge

Plastron – position of hinge

Above *Hingeback tortoises are able to shut the rear part of their shells to protect them from predators.*

environments than either the forest hingeback tortoise *(K. erosa)* or Home's hingeback tortoise *(K. homeana)* which both require very high levels of humidity. Failure to provide this will result in severe eye inflammation, possible respiratory problems and kidney disease. Hingeback tortoises which are kept too dry will remain lethargic and inactive and will refuse to feed. An occasional spray of fine mist from a hand plant sprayer is often helpful. Access to shallow, tepid water for bathing and regular soaking is absolutely critical.

Most hingeback tortoises, especially *K. erosa* and *K. homeana*, actively dislike bright light and prefer a well shaded, warm and very moist habitat. A cypress mulch and leaf-litter substrate is ideal for these species. Unlike most land tortoises, African hingeback

Above *Bell's hingeback tortoise is generally widespread throughout central and southern Africa where it prefers dry grassland habitat.*

tortoises are omnivorous and are insectivores. In the wild, their diets include snails, slugs and millipedes, as well as fallen fruits, grasses and plants. Hingeback tortoises have a reputation for being a fairly difficult species to keep, so are not ideal unless you have adequate experience.

Below *Home's hingeback tortoise. Its shell is sharply angular and falls off abruptly at the rear end.*

Choosing a healthy tortoise

If buying a tortoise in a pet store or from a breeder, do not be afraid to ask questions or to examine the animal carefully. Check any husbandry advice you are given with totally independent third parties, such as a knowledgeable friend or tortoise organisation. Observe the animals closely. There are certain indications that can be very revealing. An initial examination may show up any of the following:

The plastron and carapace should feel reasonably resilient, not 'soft' or 'spongy'. In very small juveniles, some movement is typical, but if the shell is really soft or lumpy, you should suspect a calcium or D3 deficiency problem.

Check the eyelids for swelling, exudations or redness; the eyes should be bright and unclouded. A swelling just behind the eye (on the ear) usually indicates a middle-ear infection or abscess.

Open-mouthed breathing. This can indicate that a respiratory problem is present.

Check the nares (nasal openings) for discharge. Closed or constricted nares suggest a history of chronic rhinitis ('RNS') or a possible nasal abscess.

Check the inside of mouth for anaemia, a common indicator of a heavy load of internal or external parasites. The inside of the mouth should be a healthy pale pink. Thickened saliva, ulcers or bleeding indicates an infection may be present. Brown-yellow matter on the mucous membranes or tongue is usually due to a bacterial infection known as 'mouth rot' or 'necrotic stomatitis'. This condition is highly contagious. If one animal in a group has it, you can assume that they have all been exposed.

Tortoises should feel solid rather than hollow when lifted. If you are inexperienced at handling these animals, compare with others of the same size.

If the **hind legs** are continually extended, this may mean constipation, egg retention, a severe calcium deficiency, bowel problems or bladder stones.

Above *Overcrowding tortoises can result in serious health and behavioural problems. Check any animal that you consider buying very carefully.*

We would recommend that any animal that has been wild-caught or kept with others should be tested by your veterinarian as soon as possible for parasites. It is also highly advisable to quarantine all new arrivals for at least 18 months, as tortoises can be active carriers of a range of bacterial and viral diseases without displaying any outward signs of infection. If new 'carrier' tortoises are added to an existing group, you could end up losing them all, as there are no effective treatments available at the time of writing for some of the more aggressive viral pathogens that affect tortoises.

Faecal matter adhering to the cloaca can indicate a problem with intestinal parasites, a bacterial infection, or that an incorrect diet has been provided.

Does the **shell look healthy**, like this? Ceck for any evidence of shell disease or growth deformity. Minor scute irregularities are not normally a problem.

How to sex tortoises

There are a number of external signs or characteristics that may be used to determine the sex of tortoises. However, these indicators do vary between individual species. Without a lot of practical experience, they can be quite difficult for an observer to interpret. It is also vital to realise that the sex of small tortoises and hatchlings can rarely be determined with any degree of accuracy. In some cases, sex cannot be reliably determined until the animal approaches sexual maturity. Therefore, if buying juveniles, be prepared for things to turn out rather differently from what you expected or might have been led to believe. Generally speaking, however, the following characteristics provide a pretty reliable indication, in adult animals at least:

Almost without exception, male tortoises have much longer tails than females.

Plastron

If the plastron (bottom of the shell) is curved or depressed inwards then this is a good indication that the tortoise is a male. The greatest degree of plastron concavity is seen in some tropical tortoises such as the redfoot tortoise (Geochelone carbonaria) but the same characteristic occurs to a lesser extent in the males of many species. If the plastron is entirely flat this usually indicates that the tortoise is a female. Once again, however, there are some exceptions, and no single character should be considered diagnostic by itself. If you have little experience of tortoises and are unused to comparing them, it is easy to make a mistake.

Tail length

Almost without exception, male tortoises have much longer tails than females. This is particularly clear in the case of the Hermann's tortoise (Testudo hermanni) but is also true of many other species. As a very general rule, if the tail is long enough to be carried tucked up and sideways when the tortoise walks along, it is a male; if it is short and stubby, in all probability it is a female. There are a few exceptions to this and some tortoises can be extremely difficult to sex accurately. Leopard tortoises (Geochelone pardalis) are particularly problematic in that visible external differences between males and females are not only slight but are also subject to considerable variability.

Left *It is often possible to tell the sex of tortoises by studying the body shape, tail length and plastron, as in the case of this South American redfoot tortoise. A concave plastron is strongly indicative of a male.*

Above *Almost without exception, male tortoises have much longer tails than females.*

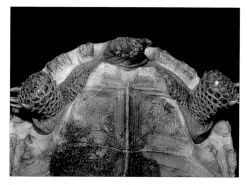

Above *A short and stubby tail generally indicates a female – but remember, the rule is not infallible.*

Above *If the underside (plastron) is curved or depressed inwards, the tortoise is probably male.*

Above *If the plastron is entirely flat, this usually indicates that the tortoise is a female.*

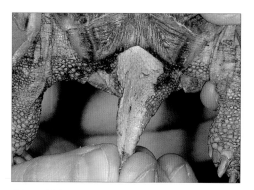

Above *Males can have a deeper V-shaped anal notch to the end of the plastron.*

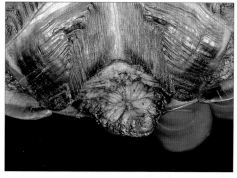

Above *The notch in the female is often shallower to make the laying of eggs easier.*

Tortoises and their environment

Tortoises are almost entirely dependent upon the environment for the heat they require to function properly. They generate almost no internal metabolic heat. Unlike a mammal, their body temperature (and hence activity level) is critically linked to their surroundings. Even the way in which the different species make use of environments varies enormously. It is important to realise that tortoises only feed under certain conditions, and most critical of these is the need for adequate light and appropriate temperatures. Most non-tropical species, such as Mediterranean tortoises, require background temperatures of around 21°C (70°F) minimum with a basking spot of around 30°C (86°F) in order to function normally. The gradient, or differential, between the high and low temperatures is important, and tortoises use this to self-regulate their body temperatures by moving from one site to another. Leopard and sulcata tortoises have very similar requirements. Species from tropical forest habitats will instead require a more or less constant temperature in the 28-29°C (82-84°F) range day and night.

This is one reason why understanding the basic biology of the species you keep is so very important. For example, a tropical species such as the

forest hingeback tortoise *(Kinixys erosa)* requires very different heating arrangements from a Mediterranean tortoise such as a Hermann's tortoise *(Testudo hermanni)*. Tropical species tend to require gentle, all-round warmth with little variation between daytime and overnight temperatures, where non-tropical species will require an overhead basking heat source with a big differential between daytime and night temperatures.

Basking behaviour

Just as it would be a mistake to keep a non-tropical species at elevated temperatures day and night, it is equally a mistake to subject tropical forest habitat species to daytime temperatures that are too high or nighttime temperatures that are too low. In both cases the animal will become severely stressed and is likely to develop serious health problems. Broadly speaking, it is possible to divide tortoises into two main groups: basking species and non-basking species. This should be viewed as a kind of 'sliding scale' of behaviour, with few species being exclusively one or the other, but fitting somewhere in between. For example, a leopard tortoise *(Geochelone pardalis)* has requirements strongly biased towards basking, whereas a redfoot tortoise *(Geochelone carbonaria)* is biased much more towards gaining heat from ambient, or background sources. These very important differences in basic requirements will have a major impact upon exactly what kind of housing and supplementary heating is required in captivity.

Above top *Keeping a tropical tortoise like the Indian star successfully in northern climates poses a challenge.*

Above *The large leopard and African spurred tortoises are adapted to warm, dry habitats. Keepers must realise that they will need warm accommodation all year round if they are to thrive.*

Left *You must make proper provision for an animal that is at home in the arid Namib desert to allow it to adjust to life in a temperate climate.*

25

Outdoor housing

Where possible, outdoor housing will provide the best quality of life for a captive tortoise. Very few tortoises are suitable for keeping as exclusively indoor pets. The more similar your own location is to the natural habitat of the species you keep, the easier it is to provide high quality outdoor housing. If you live in a region with high ambient humidity and high temperatures, you may do very well with some of the tropical species. If you live in an area with very low humidity or low temperatures, you may find keeping tropical forest species outdoors impossible. In such cases, you will certainly have to rely upon a combination of indoor and outdoor housing

Above *A well-planted outdoor pen for Mediterranean tortoises with a well-drained substrate and slopes.*

for much of the year. If you live in a region with cool, short summers and long, cold winters, you are going to find keeping tortoises much more work- (and cost-) intensive than keepers who live in warmer environments.

All pens need to be secure against two eventualities: the tortoises inside getting out, and potentially lethal predators getting in. The list of predators that can attack and kill

tortoises is quite long, and includes rats, dogs, raccoons (in the USA), badgers, hedgehogs and even large birds. In some localities, even ants can pose a significant threat. Domestic animals can also pose a threat. The Tortoise Trust receives several calls a year from people who have had their tortoise attacked, and often killed, by their family's previously well-behaved pet dog.

Securing the outer perimeter

The outer perimeters of all pens need to be of adequate height, at least twice as high as the largest tortoise is long. Corners need to be adequately secured, as many species are excellent climbers. Other species are adept at digging and burrowing. Burying a wire mesh barrier beneath ground level as part of the perimeter is highly advisable in such cases. Despite their 'slow' reputation, tortoises are really very agile creatures, as the number of tortoises reported as escaped each year to the Tortoise Trust testifies!

Below *Many species like to create their own burrows. So outdoor pens should be designed to allow this.*

Toxic Plants

Sweet pea

Anemone

Hydrangea

It cannot be assumed that tortoises will naturally avoid eating toxic plants when grazing in the garden. Keepers should therefore take care to avoid planting any potentially dangerous plants in – or nearby to – tortoise enclosures. This is not a complete list, but it does highlight those common plants that are most often associated with cases of poisoning.

Foxglove

- Aconite
- Anemone
- Azalea
- Begonia
- Bird of Paradise
- Buttercup
- Calla lily
- Cyclamen
- Daffodil
- Dianthus
- Foxglove
- Hemlock

- Hydrangea
- Ivy
- Lily of the valley
- Lobelia
- Mistletoe
- Nightshade
- Oleander
- Prunus species
- Ragwort
- Rhododendron
- Sweet pea

Daffodil

Above *It is important to protect your tortoises from unwelcome predators.*
Left *A California desert tortoise grazes in a purpose-built outdoor pen.*

Tortoise enclosure design

Flat pens on a grassy lawn are not an adequate environment for any tortoise. Non-tropical tortoises need very well drained substrates and pens should contain a variety of slopes, rocks, open basking areas, shady areas, and good provision of edible vegetation. A predator-proof overnight or poor-weather shelter should also be available. One simple design resembles a small cloche or gardener's cucumber frame. Based on a strong, rot-proof wooden frame and featuring a tough polycarbonate transparent roof, this type of unit can make a major difference to the overall health of any Mediterranean tortoise. The tortoise can enter and leave this unit at will, and it will quickly learn to use it in its daily thermoregulation cycle. In effect, this creates a mini-greenhouse, and temperatures within such a unit can easily be up to 10°C (18°F) warmer than temperatures outside. This can make a huge difference to feeding and

overall health. No artificial heat is needed, as even on wet and overcast days, this unit will be dry and warm.

Pens on dead flat surfaces are not attractive to tortoises as they much prefer a sloping or undulating topography. If a tortoise falls upon its back on a dead flat and smooth surface, it may have difficulty righting itself, whereas on a sloped, rough surface with vegetation cover they can usually 'flip' themselves over rapidly.

Mediterranean tortoises

It is absolutely vital that Mediterranean or other semi-arid habitat tortoises are maintained on well-drained substrates. Damp, saturated clay-type substrates will contribute to an increased incidence of shell infections, especially on the plastron (underside) and also to increased likelihood of serious respiratory conditions. Aim for a mix of loose, sandy-type soils for all *Testudo* species.

Many people greatly underestimate the effect that the correct choice of substrate has on the overall health of tortoises. In many cases, it can make the difference between long-term survival and a life plagued by infections.

Provide shade and shelter

A well-planted pen of adequate size can also be largely self-supporting in terms of food provision, permitting grazing at will on a high-fibre, healthy diet of mixed flowers, herbs and miscellaneous edible 'weeds'. Plants also provide hiding places and shade. Our own pens have been designed to meet both needs. Additional shade is provided by

Above *A tortoise that falls on its back in a flat enclosure will struggle to right itself. It is better to design pens with slopes and plentiful plant cover.*

Above *Plants provide welcome areas of shade in an outdoor pen.*

Above *A well-drained substrate suits Mediterranean tortoises.*

Left *A planted outdoor pen with edible vegetation and shelters.*

use of half-buried hollowed-out logs, and by plastic pots or buckets cut in half and partially buried. These allow the tortoises to retreat to a stable microclimate in case of very hot or very cold weather, just as they would retreat to their scrapes or burrows in the wild.

Tropical tortoises

The outdoor requirements for tropical tortoises are quite different, and highly dependent upon your own location. Species from humid environments will require very special housing in cool and dry climates. The larger species such

as redfoot and yellowfoot tortoises are especially challenging, as not only do they require specialised climates, they also require a lot of space. Many keepers of these species maintain a large tropical house with year-round heating and humidity control. This obviously requires a substantial financial investment initially, and ongoing running costs are also high. This is one reason why we suggest very careful consideration before making a commitment to keep species like this. Of course, if you live in a semi-tropical location yourself, then you may find that you can successfully maintain these species relatively easily.

Indoor housing

Even Mediterranean tortoises that may be successfully maintained out of doors for much of the year may require indoor housing from time to time, whether as juveniles, or as adults, in particularly poor weather. Good quality indoor accommodation may also be needed when tortoises are emerging from hibernation or if over-wintering a sick tortoise.

We at the Tortoise Trust do not recommend the use of glass vivarium 'tanks' for tortoises under any circumstances. This type of enclosure is far from ideal in a number of ways. They offer very limited floor space and poor ventilation. It is extremely difficult to achieve an adequate temperature gradient in this type of enclosure. In addition, tortoises respond badly to housing in glass tanks from a behavioural perspective. They will constantly try to walk through the walls, often bruising themselves in the process. We have noted a very high incidence of accelerated growth and 'lumpy shell' problems in tortoises raised in glass vivaria, as well as unacceptably high rates of respiratory disease.

Make your own tortoise table

As an effective alternative, we have, for many years now, been using open-topped 'tortoise tables' for maintaining juveniles indoors, and similarly equipped larger open-topped indoor pens in the case of larger animals. These provide a very good quality environment and our results over the past 20 years using this method have been excellent. They are far easier to maintain than glass tanks, and have the added advantage of being much safer. In addition, they are easy to custom build to fit to any available space at relatively low cost.

Housing systems of this type are easily constructed at home, or for small tortoises, ready-made containers such as under-bed storage units or agricultural-type plastic tubs can quickly be adapted. Tortoises kept in units of this type receive good ventilation and the substrate (usually a mixture of sand and soil) also tends to remain very dry which is another important advantage as damp substrates are associated with skin, shell and respiratory disease in arid-habitat species.

Seed tray filled with cobbles for clambering over

Covered section to provide shade if sited in a sunny room

Frame constructed from wooden floorboards

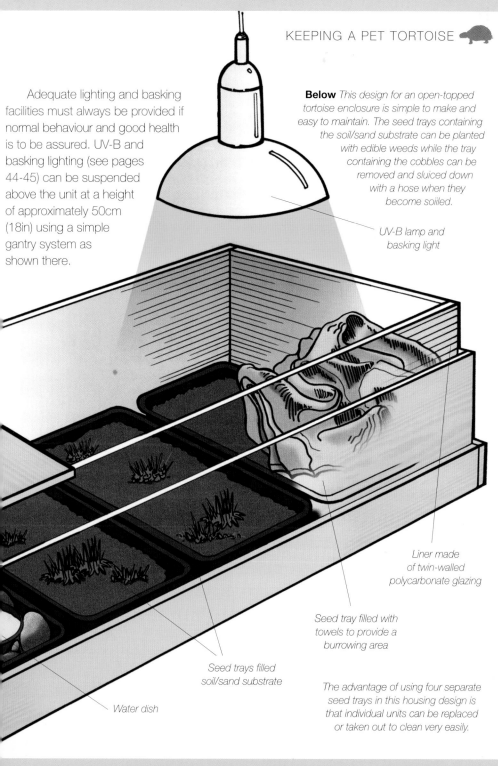

Adequate lighting and basking facilities must always be provided if normal behaviour and good health is to be assured. UV-B and basking lighting (see pages 44-45) can be suspended above the unit at a height of approximately 50cm (18in) using a simple gantry system as shown there.

Below *This design for an open-topped tortoise enclosure is simple to make and easy to maintain. The seed trays containing the soil/sand substrate can be planted with edible weeds while the tray containing the cobbles can be removed and sluiced down with a hose when they become soiled.*

UV-B lamp and basking light

Liner made of twin-walled polycarbonate glazing

Seed tray filled with towels to provide a burrowing area

Seed trays filled soil/sand substrate

Water dish

The advantage of using four separate seed trays in this housing design is that individual units can be replaced or taken out to clean very easily.

Indoor tropical tortoise accommodation

In captivity, the provision of appropriate high humidity environments for certain tropical species (for example, redfoot, yellowfoot and hingeback tortoises) can prove problematic. The failure to provide such environments, however, can have extremely serious consequences, as these species are very susceptible to environmentally induced dehydration. Some consequences of this include kidney failure, skin problems and eye problems. Typical centrally heated houses reveal relative humidity levels as low as 20 per cent in winter, which is far too low for tropical species from humid habitats. Some books recommend 'adding a dish of water in the terrarium' as a solution, but such measures are almost totally inadequate. Much more effective measures are necessary to achieve satisfactory levels.

Unfortunately, humidifying an entire room to adequate levels for most tropical forest-dwelling tortoises (28°C/82°F at around 80 per cent relative humidity) is rarely practical, and would probably result in structural damage and damage to furnishings. Such levels certainly can be achieved if you have a tropical greenhouse, but for most keepers it is far more practical to restrict the animals to a smaller, properly treated enclosure. This is relatively easy to achieve in the case of smaller species, such as hingeback tortoises, or in the case of juveniles of larger species.

One simple method that can work very well in such cases is to use a large plastic

For most keepers it is far more practical to restrict the animals to a smaller, properly treated enclosure.

tub with the addition of a warm-air-type humidifier next to the unit. The top should be partially covered with a sheet of twin-walled polycarbonate material (available from builders' merchants and large DIY stores). This is much easier and lighter to handle (and clean) than a glass tank-type vivarium and is also far safer around the house, being practically unbreakable. You can also achieve a substantial amount of internal floor space at moderate expense with a simple unit like this. Do make sure that the rest of the room is well-ventilated and that the background heat is adequate. Failure to do this will result in damaging condensation forming. We do not recommend ultrasonic humidifiers for tropical tortoises as the mist they produce is rather cold. Always choose a 'warm-air' type. *continued*

Above *A converted greenhouse can provide good quality accommodation for tropical tortoises.*

Right *A large plastic tub can be converted into suitable housing for small or juvenile tropical tortoises with the addition of a humidifier.*

Twin-walled polycarbonate sheet

Warm-air type humidifier

Large diameter hose from humidifier

Plastic tub

Left *A mister that produces a fine 'rain' of water droplets can be used in conjunction with a humidifer.*

Below *The tropical eroded hingeback tortoise.*

Left *This lush rainforest is the natural habitat of some tropical tortoises that live in humid environments.*

Indoor tropical tortoise accommodation

Heat and light

Gentle local heating can be provided by means of heat mats directly under the tub, and a non-toxic, moist orchid bark and sphagnum moss substrate will serve to create a very realistic 'tropical forest' habitat and microclimate. Most of these species prefer to avoid very bright lighting, and their basking behaviour is much reduced compared to desert and savannah species, – nevertheless, some basking provision should be made. In most cases an overhead ceramic heater controlled by a thermostat is ideal for this kind of environment. Most tropical forest species acquire at least some of their vitamin D3 requirement from animal prey or from carrion in the wild. High intensity UV-B lighting is not required. Instead, a lower level UV-B source and some oral supplementation is more than adequate.

Arid habitat species

Tropical arid habitat tortoises are somewhat easier to maintain indoors if we exclude the fact that many of these are rather large. Leopard tortoises, sulcata tortoises and Indian star tortoises, for example, will do very well in almost identical conditions to those required when keeping Mediterranean tortoises indoors. A large, brightly lit pen with a dry substrate and an overhead combined UV-B-Heat (self-ballasted mercury vapour) basking source is ideal. Do remember to provide regular soaks and fresh drinking water, however, as even these semi-arid habitat species can suffer the consequences of chronic dehydration if this is not available.

Above *Tortoises from arid habitats benefit from the provision of a UV-B-Heat basking source. These lamps look like regular spot basking lamps but they also emit significant levels of essential UV-B.*

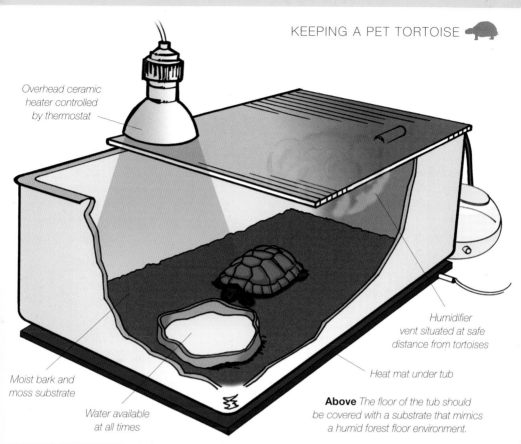

Overhead ceramic
heater controlled
by thermostat

Humidifier
vent situated at safe
distance from tortoises

Heat mat under tub

Moist bark and
moss substrate

Water available
at all times

Above *The floor of the tub should
be covered with a substrate that mimics
a humid forest floor environment.*

Above *Do take care – tortoises
that fall on their backs under a
heat source can rapidly die.*

Left *It is vital to provide water
both to drink and soak in.*

Dietary requirements

The diets demanded by different species vary considerably. Some species (typically those from rainforest habitats) are omnivorous, and may require fruit in their diets. In the case of other species, the inclusion of fruit or animal protein is highly damaging. Some species require very high fibre mixed grass diets, while other species need flowers and leaves exclusively. Finding a regular supply of suitable foods can be challenging and expensive, especially in winter. More detailed advice about feeding is given on the following pages but do also research the feeding habits of the species you are interested in well in advance. You must be able to provide exactly what is needed on a reliable basis.

Do not make the common mistake of thinking that tortoises can just be left alone to graze on a lawn, or that you can buy all the food you will need from pet stores. Neither is true. Many keepers find they have to grow the foods required from seed. Make sure that you have the facilities and time to do this. Nutritional mismanagement is one of the biggest killers of captive tortoises. Juveniles, especially, are highly sensitive to even small imbalances in nutrition and there is little room for error. This is one area of husbandry that you simply cannot afford to get wrong. Each species has very particular requirements, as we have already noted, but most can usefully be divided into one of several groups.

It is vital that the diet is tailored exactly to suit the species you are keeping.

An ideal diet
Some of the key factors that must be considered when making up an 'ideal' diet for a tortoise are:
- Protein level
- Fibre content
- Calcium to phosphorus balance
- Fruit content (only for certain species)
- Miscellaneous trace element content
- Water content
- Animal protein content (if any, only for naturally omnivorous species)

It is vital that the diet is tailored exactly to suit the species you are keeping and you should avoid relying on non-specific, generalised feeding advice. It is not possible to simply employ one 'tortoise diet' that is suitable or safe for all species, and nowhere is this more true than in the case of commercial dried foods that may be recommended to you. These products may appear to offer an

Above *Correct nutrition is vital for your tortoise's well-being. Take time to find out about the correct diet.*

easy solution to the feeding problem, but our experience of them is that they leave much to be desired and are no real substitute for a varied diet based upon the natural feeding behaviour of a particular tortoise.

One very important point is how much to feed. Unfortunately, the answer to this will depend upon many different factors including the size and age of the tortoise, the species involved, and especially upon the temperatures it is kept at. High food intakes will produce much more rapid growth than more modest intakes. High growth rates are not necessarily desirable, however. Feeding the correct amount is a matter of balancing the need for sufficient nutrition while avoiding overfeeding. As there are so many variables, we recommend seeking specific advice from a reputable tortoise group or specialist vet.

Above *Herbivorous tortoises should be provided with a wide range of leaves, flowers and fruits, selected for the species.*

Top *Feed natural 'weeds' rather than shop-bought lettuce which is deficient in vitamins and fibre.*

Left *Take care with fruit – some species can tolerate it but others may suffer gastric upsets.*

Feeding Mediterranean and Russian tortoises

The diet of Mediterranean and Russian tortoises in the wild consists almost entirely of herbaceous and succulent vegetation and flowers. During periods of rainfall, the tortoise will drink from the puddles which form, and it may also approach streams or ponds. It will frequently also pass urine at this time as well, and will simultaneously dispose of the chalky white uric acid residues which form in the bladder. It is categorically not true that wild tortoises rarely drink. During the dry season, and in the more arid parts of their range, tortoises rely mainly upon the water content of their food in order to supply their moisture needs (if they are active at all), but invariably drink enthusiastically whenever it does rain. In captivity, we suggest soaking the tortoise for 10 minutes twice each week (up to about chin height) in fresh, shallow water.

Left *A regular soak in a tub of shallow water helps to keep tortoises hydrated.*

Leaves and flowers

In captivity, a high-fibre, low-protein and calcium-rich diet will ensure good digestive tract function and smooth shell growth. Such a diet will be based around fresh green leaves and edible flowers. The more variety the better. Mediterranean and Russian tortoises fed on cat or dog food, or other high-protein food items such as peas or beans, frequently die from kidney failure or from impacted bladder stones consisting of solidified urates.

Peas and beans are also very high in phytic acid which, like oxalic acid, inhibits calcium uptake. Avoid reliance upon 'supermarket' greens and fruits which may contain inadequate fibre levels, excessive pesticide residues, and are too rich in sugar. Fruit should be given very sparingly as it can lead to diarrhoea, intestinal parasite proliferation and colic. *continued*

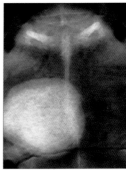

Left *Fruits like tomatoes should only be given sparingly.*

Above *An X-ray of a bladder stone caused by dehydration and a diet too high in protein.*

Below *Fresh water should always be readily available.*

Below *In the wild these tortoises eat leaves and grasses.*

Feeding Mediterranean and Russian tortoises

Although these tortoises will take animal protein if offered (as will most normally herbivorous tortoises), in practice this leads to excessive growth and causes shell deformities, liver disease, and renal stress. It should therefore be avoided entirely.

A balanced diet for such tortoises can also include dandelion, naturally occurring non-toxic weeds, white (Dutch) clover, rose leaves and petals, and sow-thistle, romaine or red leaf lettuce (in very limited quantities). Do not use head lettuces, such as iceberg, as these contain little in the way of vitamins or minerals.

Most herbivorous tortoises fare best when allowed to graze naturally, offering the other listed items as occasional supplements. Do not routinely offer cabbage, spinach, chard, bok choy, or any vegetable related to these, as they inhibit calcium absorption and can cause health problems. This is particularly critical in the case of juveniles or egg-laying females.

The regular use of a cuttlefish bone left in the enclosures allows tortoises to regulate the amount of calcium in the diet.

Allowing Mediterranean tortoises to forage and graze naturally actually helps the tortoise to maintain good digestive-tract health, and greatly assists in the prevention of obesity. If scute pyramiding is noted, this usually indicates that either too much of the 'right' type of food is being consumed, or,

more likely, that the overall protein content of the diet is too high. We recommend the use of a good quality phosphorus-free calcium and vitamin D3 supplement at least twice per week and more frequently for juveniles and egg-laying females.

Above and left *Red leaf lettuce and romaine are better options than a variety like iceberg which is not very nutritious.*

Below *Placing cuttlefish bone in the pen can provide a useful extra source of calcium and helps keep beaks in shape.*

Left *The leaves, stems and flowers of white clover are all suitable for feeding to Russian and Mediterranean tortoises. Be careful, however, to avoid picking plants that may have been sprayed with chemicals or been contaminated by the emissions from vehicle exhausts.*

Above *The pyramiding on the shell of this radiated tortoise from Madagascar shows what can happen if a tortoise is fed an incorrect diet.*

Left *This mixture of flowers and leaves is an ideal diet for a Mediterranean tortoise. Under no circumstances should animal protein, or other high protein, high fat foods be provided.*

Tropical tortoise diets

Some tropical tortoises have dietary requirements that are similar to Mediterranean species, but others have highly specialised diets that perfectly suit what is available in their particular habitat. It is extremely important to know what your tortoise is adapted to eating in the wild, and then to structure the captive diet around this.

'meadow hay' and 'orchard hay' mixes (which can be obtained from specialist pet suppliers) are usually suitable. Avoid hays that have excessively 'prickly' seed heads – these can injure mouths or eyes. Second or third cuttings of grass hays tend to have less spiny heads than first cuttings. This grass-based primary diet should be supplemented with flowers as frequently as possible (hibiscus, dandelion, petunia, etc.). De-spined *Opuntia* pads, clovers and other fodder 'weeds' listed previously should also be included on a regular basis. As always, pay attention in addition to calcium and vitamin D3 requirements if problems with bone formation are to be avoided.

Feeding leopard, sulcata and Indian star tortoises

For large savannah species, such as *Geochelone sulcata* (African spurred tortoise) or *Geochelone pardalis* (leopard tortoise), grasses and hays are a critical dietary component. Some other species also benefit from the inclusion of both fresh and dried grasses in their diet, for example, Indian star tortoises. It should be noted that certain species, such as redfoot, yellowfoot, hingeback and Mediterranean tortoises, are ill-equipped to digest the high silica content of grass fodder. For species adapted to it, however, grass is not only nutritious, but its fibre content makes a significant contribution to digestive health. For leopard and African spurred tortoises, mixed grasses should comprise approximately 70-75 per cent of the total diet.

The availability of grass types varies greatly according to location, but general

Feeding hingeback, redfoot and yellowfoot tortoises

These tortoises are omnivorous to a greater or lesser extent depending upon species. Some low-fat animal protein should be included in the diet of these species. We recommend re-hydrating dried cat food in a tub with additional minerals and vitamins as a safe and suitable source of animal protein. We provide about 25g (1oz) of moist cat food to a fully grown (10kg/22lb) redfoot tortoise on a weekly basis, with proportionally less for juveniles. Green-leaf vegetation and edible flowers should make up the bulk of the diet. Fruits are also part of the diet of these species in the wild, and unlike leopard or African spurred tortoises, their digestive tract copes easily with this richer, sweeter intake. They all tend to prefer over-ripened fruits, including banana, mango, papaya, strawberry and edible mushroom.

This same basic diet seems to suit hingebacks, which are also highly omnivorous in nature, and approximately 5-10g (0.2-0.4oz) of animal protein per week is appropriate in this case. It is also important to note that these tortoises, if allowed access to a damp, moist garden or well-vegetated tropical house, will usually find slugs and snails for themselves. It is extremely important to avoid the use of slug pellets or other toxic chemicals in any garden where tortoises are kept. Millipedes and similar invertebrates also constitute an important part of the diet of hingeback tortoises in nature.

Above *The tropical rroded hingeback tortoise,*

Above and left *Slugs, snails and millipedes from the garden will all be happily consumed by hingeback tortoises which are omnivorous by nature.*

Above *Leopard tortoises graze extensively upon mixed grasses. They also favour the fruit and pads of the prickly pear, succulents and thistles. In captivity it is a common error to feed too much 'wet' food, such as lettuce, tomatoes and fruit.*

Vitamin D3 and UV-B lighting

Vitamin D3 is a fat-soluble vitamin, which means that it can be stored in the body for long periods of time. It is acquired either through the UV-B component of sunlight or diet, or both. When the tortoise's skin is exposed to the sun, through basking for example, the vitamin D production process is initiated. Vitamin D3 is considered to be both a vitamin and a prohormone because of its action with a chemical called 7-dehydrocholesterol. Ultraviolet rays in sunlight act on oils in the skin, and in a process which also requires radiant heat, produce the pre-vitamin D, which is then absorbed into the body. This is then metabolised in the liver, and then converted again in the kidneys into an activated form. It then returns to the intestinal mucosal cells, where it begins the production of a calcium-binding protein needed for the absorption of calcium from the diet.

Left *This skin of tortoises is naturally quite rich in oils.*

> When the tortoise's skin is exposed to the sun, through basking for example, the vitamin D process is initiated

Even if there is adequate calcium in the diet, it will not be absorbed unless Vitamin D3 levels are adequate.

In order to produce natural vitamin D3 from sunlight, unfiltered exposure must be provided, as even window glass will block the essential UV-B spectrum. That is why outdoor basking is so vital to tortoises. Cloud cover will also reduce UV-B levels, and generally UV-B levels are far lower in northern latitudes than they are at the equator or in areas where tortoises live in the wild. As a general rule, if you live in an area where tortoises and turtles occur naturally and your animals are able to spend at least three or four hours outdoors in unfiltered sunlight daily, you probably do not need to rely upon oral D3 supplements. A calcium supplement alone should suffice. If you live in a northern, cloudy area where tortoises and turtles do not occur naturally, or your animals' outdoor time is restricted, it is recommended that you do use a supplement on a regular basis. This is why knowledgeable tortoise keepers place so much importance on artificial UV-B lighting, and on carefully formulated calcium and vitamin D3 oral supplementation.

Catering for plant eaters

Omnivorous tortoises get a high proportion of their vitamin D3 requirement from their food. Plants do not contain D3, however, but instead contain vitamin D2, which is far less efficient in terms of calcium metabolism than D3. Herbivorous tortoises kept indoors are, therefore, far more dependent upon the quantity and quality of artificial lighting than omnivorous species.

A number of specialist lamps are available that will help a tortoise to generate vitamin D3. These include so-called 'full spectrum' fluorescent tubes with UV-B output that is usually expressed as a percentage (2%, 5% and 8% tubes are most common), with a higher number indicating a higher output. In order to be effective, these tubes need to be no more than about 50cm (24in) from the tortoise, and there should no intervening glass or mesh. The output of such tubes also diminishes over time, so they should be changed every six months.

Another option are so-called 'UV-Heat' lamps based upon a self-ballasted mercury vapour construction. These are especially effective as not only do they have high levels of UV-B output, they also produce heat, and, as we have seen, heat is essential to the D3 production cycle.

They last much longer than fluorescent tubes, sustaining an adequate output for 18 months or more. They are the recommended source of light and heat for all basking species.

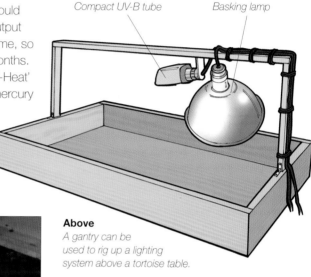

Compact UV-B tube   *Basking lamp*

Above
A gantry can be used to rig up a lighting system above a tortoise table.

Left *These herbivorous tortoises are feeding under a basking lamp and a UV-B tube.*

Above *Basking in the sun causes the vitamin D production process to get under way.*

Using food supplements

Captive diets rarely approach the range and quality of what a tortoise feeds on in the wild. The Hermann's tortoise, for example, naturally browses on over 150 different varieties of leaves and flowers, grazed over a very large area. They also gnaw on small pieces of discarded snail shells, and have been observed to pick at tufa limestone rocks. The net result is that they gain access to an extraordinarily wide range of mineral trace elements and enjoy a calcium-rich diet with high levels of UV-B exposure via sunshine.

Above *Applying a dietary supplement to the food of a group of herbivorous tortoises.*

By contrast, most captive diets are far more restricted in variety, and the plants that are available are unlikely to have been grown in soils that have the same kind of mineral balance as the tortoise's natural habitat.

One of the most common nutrition-related health problems of captive tortoises (and turtles) is metabolic bone disease, a condition closely related to osteoporosis and rickets in humans. The underlying cause is a diet inadequate in calcium and vitamin D3.

The condition is most frequent and severe in hatchlings and juveniles as it is during periods of rapid growth that any lack of bone-building 'raw materials' is most critical. Egg-laying females are also at considerable risk if their diet is in any way deficient.

The best way to prevent such problems is by making sure that the base diet is correctly tailored for the species in question, and by using a specially formulated multi-mineral and vitamin supplement on a daily basis. Such products are available from veterinary surgeons or from specialist reptile suppliers. Aim for a supplement that has a minimum calcium to phosphorus ratio of 2:1 (although studies of tortoise diets in the wild suggest that a higher ratio is preferable). Some formulations are 'phosphorus free' and these are ideal in many ways as the phosphorus requirement will easily be met from the diet itself, whereas calcium needs are much harder to accommodate from food alone.

Problem foods

Another problem in relying exclusively upon diet alone to provide for all mineral requirements is that many plants that on the surface appear to offer good, or positive calcium-to-phosphorus ratios, also contain certain chemicals that inhibit calcium utilisation. Mustard greens, turnip greens, kale, cabbage, bok choy, spinach, chard and collard greens all fall into this category. One of the best known examples of such an 'anti-nutrient factor' is oxalic acid. Another is phytic acid, found in high concentrations in peas, beans and related legumes. These are all items that should be excluded as regular parts of the diet of herbivorous tortoises, although occasional use will not cause any harm.

It is also vitally important to avoid over-rapid growth in hatchlings and juveniles. This places huge demands on the calcium metabolism that are hard to support. Slow, even growth is much better for long-term health and survival than accelerated growth. Over-rapid growth can be prevented by carefully monitoring the diet to prevent over consumption of protein-rich items, and by preventing general over-feeding.

Above *This young Hermann's tortoise (*Testudo hermanni*) displays a very obvious growth ring (the paler band around the carapace).*

Below *A smooth, domed shell, typical of growth on a good diet. The correct diet contributes greatly to proper shell growth.*

Right *An African spurred tortoise (*Geochelone sulcata*), displaying the deformed shell typical of metabolic bone disease.*

Tips

- Try to provide a diet that provides an overall positive calcium-to-phosphorus ratio.

- Do not rely on foods high in oxalates, phytates or other calcium-inhibiting compounds.

- Use a phosphorus-free calcium supplement daily.

- Carefully consider vitamin D3 requirements. Provide access to adequate levels of natural sunlight, use an adequate and correctly installed and maintained artificial UV-B source, or provide an oral D3 supplement at least three times per week.

- Provide a general broad spectrum mineral trace element supplement once per week.

Captive breeding

Many keepers are interested in the possibility of breeding their tortoises in captivity. Years ago, this was considered quite a feat, and was far from routine. Much less was known about hatchling care, and so even people who successfully hatched eggs found great difficulty in keeping the babies alive and raising them to adulthood. Fortunately, things have changed dramatically, and now many keepers enjoy regular breeding successes with a wide range of species. There are some very basic rules to follow if you wish to achieve sustained captive breeding success.

Above *A pair of marginated tortoises indulge in pre-mating behaviour. For the best chances of success, breeding pairs should be closely matched.*

Compatible pairs

Make absolutely certain that you only allow fully compatible pairs to mate. In many cases, unsuccessful breeders do not have compatible pairs to begin with. On no account mix species (you know that already, hopefully), but for best breeding success you need to take it much further than that.

Ideally, the pair should be as near identical in appearance as possible. The real object is to have animals from the same geographical locality. It is not enough to say that 'they are both *Testudo hermanni*, so that is close enough'. It is clear that there are quite possibly numerous genetic variations within that species complex, and the closer the visual match, the better the chances of a genetic match. There is no doubt that animals which are a close genetic match tend to be the most successful from the breeding point of view. This applies to practically all species.

Age and health

It is vital that breeding stock is in first-rate condition. Do not try to breed from animals with a recent history of poor health. Avoid trying to breed from elderly females. Not only is this unlikely to be very successful, but it also places them in serious danger. Elderly females can become stressed by the constant attentions of amorous males and have high rates of follicular stasis and egg peritonitis (two potentially fatal conditions that can develop in female tortoises that are in less than perfect breeding condition). It is also critical that breeding tortoises receive a good diet, and that their trace element needs are adequately met. Daily use of a quality multi-mineral and vitamin supplement is recommended.

Temporary separation of males and females

This is another technique that is well known to experienced breeders. Separating the males for a few weeks and then reintroducing them to the female can greatly increase their level of interest. Allowing some inter-male aggression to occur also appears to help. Do ensure that any aggression is monitored carefully, especially in the case of *Testudo marginata*, *Testudo ibera* and *Testudo hermanni*, however. These particular species can cause serious damage to each other if it gets out of control.

Temperatures

In order to breed successfully, tortoises must have access to a certain range of temperatures. This has major implications with regard to hormone

Above *A mating pair of redfoot tortoises. Female redfoot tortoises seem to prefer making their nests in very wet, almost muddy substrates.*

Right *An impressive sight – African spurred tortoises mating.*

levels, the formation and development of sperm, etc. In Northern locations, adequate temperatures are very difficult to achieve without some artificial support. It is especially important for breeding purposes that adequate levels are achieved in March-April-May as Spring is a key period in the breeding cycle. The best solution, in our own experience, is a large greenhouse or polytunnel. This will dramatically increase daytime temperatures and really does make a huge difference to breeding results. We have known many, many cases where the simple provision of a greenhouse or polytunnel has totally transformed breeding results.

Nest site availability

It is essential that all females are provided with satisfactory nesting facilities (indoors or outdoors). Failure to provide adequate nesting sites in captivity can have serious consequences for health, including an increased danger of egg-retention. An absence of acceptable nesting sites can also lead to increased stress, and can negatively impact upon captive breeding success. For example, Mediterranean *Testudo* species tend to exhibit a strong preference for nesting on gentle slopes, with sandy, well-drained soils. Damp clay soils or soil that is too stony is likely to be rejected as unsuitable, as are nest sites on flat surfaces.

Above *Once the eggs have been laid, the female will cover the clutch by scraping substrate over them.*

By contrast, many tropical species such as redfoot tortoises *(Geochelone carbonaria)* will accept flat nest sites readily, but typically prefer the soil to be rich in organic content, moist, or even muddy. Mediterranean *Testudo* species usually prefer to lay in full sun, on a dry day, from midday to late afternoon; other species, such as redfoot tortoises frequently lay at dusk, and especially during episodes of light rain when humidity is particularly high. It is important to be aware of these traits, as the prevailing weather conditions or time of day can give a good general indication as to when nesting may occur. There is no fixed 'gestation time' in tortoises, but on average nesting follows six to ten weeks after successful fertilisation.

Sufficient depth of substrate

The depth of substrate available is a very important factor for all species that excavate nests. If insufficient depth is available, nesting will usually be terminated. In captive situations, therefore, it is necessary to ensure that the laying area provides enough depth of substrate to avoid this. It is only possible to offer general guidelines, as different species do vary in their nest depths. For most species the depth of substrate should be at least equal to the length of the hind limbs plus 70 per cent of the length of the carapace. Once laid, allow the female to bury the eggs, using her hind limbs, then when she has finished gently remove them to an artificial incubator as described below. Do not interrupt her during the laying or covering up process as this can cause severe stress and can cause her to retain her eggs.

Egg incubation

Do not rely upon the old 'hit or miss' method of using an airing cupboard or overhead light bulb to incubate eggs. Instead, invest in a suitable professional standard incubator. It is vital that safe temperatures are maintained throughout the often lengthy incubation

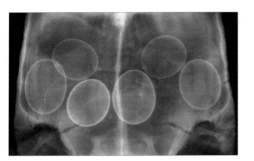

Above *An X-ray showing eggs about to be laid.*

Right *Female tortoises excavate a nest using their back legs to shovel away the substrate.*

Below *Eggs in an incubator on vermiculite substrate.*

period, which can be well over 200 days in the case of some species, such as leopard tortoises. Mediterranean tortoise eggs typically hatch in 75-85 days depending upon the exact incubation temperature employed.

In order to develop properly, tortoise eggs need to be incubated within a specific temperature and humidity range. The incubation temperature is especially critical. If the eggs are incubated at too low a temperature, development will be very slow or the eggs may fail to hatch. Excessively high temperatures can lead to deformity or death. For best results always use a reliable thermostat and thermometer when incubating eggs.

We suggest that you should avoid sand as an incubation substrate. It does not allow sufficient gaseous exchange to occur. As a result, embryonic anoxia causing 'dead in shell' babies is a real danger. It is better to use an artificial, lighter medium, such as very slightly moist vermiculite. Place the probe of a thermometer alongside the eggs to keep a constant check on conditions.

The time of incubation and the eventual sex of the offspring are both determined by temperature. Higher temperatures produce females in most species, and lower temperatures males. Suggested incubation temperatures for most species range from 29.5°C to 31.5°C (85 to 88.7°F).

Hatchling care

Young tortoises are entirely independent from the moment they hatch. Occasionally one hatches while still retaining a remnant of its yolk-sac which sustained it through the incubation period. This can be quite large and is attached the underside, thus preventing mobility. These are best left quietly in the incubator for 24 hours or so while the yolk-sac is gradually absorbed. For comprehensive data on all aspects of captive breeding (including advanced level guidance on incubation and captive care) you are advised to consult the Tortoise Trust website which has precise incubation and hatchling care guidelines for a wide range of species.

Do not make the mistake of believing the common myth that baby tortoises 'must be kept indoors for the first three years'.

An attractively landscaped open-topped enclosure provides both security and a stimulating, well-ventilated environment. Their dietary management is also exactly as for adults, but with increased sensitivity to calcium and vitamin D3 deficiencies. The prevention of unnaturally accelerated growth is especially important, as this can result not only in 'lumpy shell' and other deformities, but also in an increased risk of kidney disease and premature sexual maturity. The provision of a correctly balanced diet from day one is therefore absolutely vital.

Suitable enclosures for juveniles

Juveniles may be maintained out of doors in protected, secure enclosures whenever the weather permits, or indoors in open-topped pens. Usually a combination of both is required. Juveniles do not respond well to enclosed vivarium 'tank'-type housing. It is important to stress that juveniles require exactly the same temperatures and environments as adults of the species. Do not make the mistake of believing the common myth that baby tortoises 'must be kept indoors for the first three years'. That is completely false and is extremely damaging to their health and long-term survival prospects.

Above An infant spur-thighed tortoise breaks out of its shell. It first pierces the shell by using an egg-tooth.

Below Juvenile tortoises are at risk from dehydration so it is essential that they have access to fresh water.

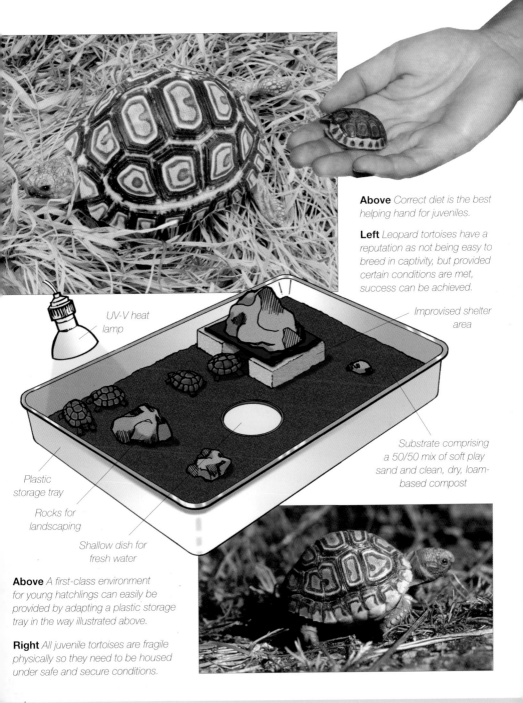

Above *Correct diet is the best helping hand for juveniles.*

Left *Leopard tortoises have a reputation as not being easy to breed in captivity, but provided certain conditions are met, success can be achieved.*

UV-V heat lamp

Improvised shelter area

Substrate comprising a 50/50 mix of soft play sand and clean, dry, loam-based compost

Plastic storage tray

Rocks for landscaping

Shallow dish for fresh water

Above *A first-class environment for young hatchlings can easily be provided by adapting a plastic storage tray in the way illustrated above.*

Right *All juvenile tortoises are fragile physically so they need to be housed under safe and secure conditions.*

Hibernation

The following information applies to the most common species of tortoises kept as pets: *Testudo graeca* (the Mediterranean spur-thighed tortoise), *Testudo hermanni* (the Hermann's tortoise), *Testudo marginata* (the marginated tortoise) and *Testudo horsfieldii* (the Russian tortoise). All of these species hibernate in the wild, with some local exceptions, and can safely do so in captivity provided certain rules are followed.

Aestivation and hotter climates

The exceptions to hibernation in the case of Mediterranean tortoises include populations which live in regions which experience very mild winters, such as southern Morocco and Spain, or the coastal regions of Tunisia and Libya. In these areas, winter daytime temperatures often exceed 20°C/70°F (and can reach 28°C/82°F). Tortoises remain fully active and feeding all winter under these conditions. These same regions also experience exceptionally hot and dry summers. In southern Morocco, for example, daytime temperatures in July can exceed 48°C (118°F). These high temperatures, and the almost total lack of plants suitable for grazing, result in aestivation. The tortoises bury themselves underground and sit out the unbearable heat, expending as little energy as possible. Although superficially similar to hibernation, aestivation is biologically a very different process and the two should not be confused. They are only similar in the sense that they result in a seasonal period of inactivity.

Above *Tortoises excrete semi-solid urates, as do birds. All food must have passed through the gastro-intestinal tract before the onset of hibernation.*

Non-hibernating species

Species that should never be hibernated include *Testudo kleinmanni* (the Egyptian tortoise) and *Testudo nabeulensis* (the Tunisian tortoise) and **all** tropical tortoises including redfoot tortoises (*Geochelone carbonaria*), African spurred tortoises (*Geochelone sulcata*), leopard tortoises (*Geochelone pardalis*), Indian star tortoises (*Geochelone elegans*) and hingeback tortoises (*Kinixys* species).

Do not attempt to hibernate any tortoise if it has eaten recently.

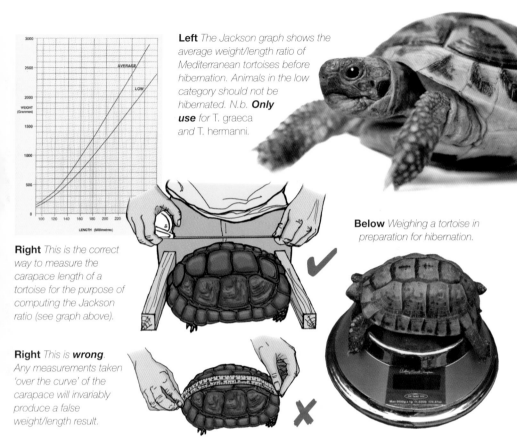

Left *The Jackson graph shows the average weight/length ratio of Mediterranean tortoises before hibernation. Animals in the low category should not be hibernated. N.b.* **Only use** *for* T. graeca *and* T. hermanni.

Right *This is the correct way to measure the carapace length of a tortoise for the purpose of computing the Jackson ratio (see graph above).*

Right *This is* **wrong**. *Any measurements taken 'over the curve' of the carapace will invariably produce a false weight/length result.*

Below *Weighing a tortoise in preparation for hibernation.*

It is natural for tortoises to gradually reduce their food intake as autumn approaches. A tortoise's digestive system is governed to a great extent by temperature, but, generally speaking, when the animal's biological processes are slowing down it takes between two to four weeks for the food last consumed to pass completely through the gastro-intestinal tract (the exact time taken depends upon the size of the tortoise; small animals require less fasting time, larger animals need a longer period). In other words, do not attempt to hibernate any tortoise if it has eaten recently. Throughout the fasting period, keep the tortoise at moderate room temperatures – above 10°C (50°F) but below 18°C (65°F). Gradually reduce lighting levels simultaneously to prepare the animal for hibernation.

Delay the start of hibernation rather than allow a tortoise to hibernate while the possibility of undigested food matter within the stomach remains. Tortoises which are hibernated with undigested food still remaining inside are unlikely to survive in good health. The food decays, produces large quantities of gas, and can cause potentially fatal colic.

Hibernation – outdoors or indoors?

Outdoor or natural hibernation consists of allowing the tortoise to excavate its own burrow instead of hibernating it in a box under controlled conditions. In the wild tortoises usually dig themselves in under large rocks, tree roots, or into the side of earthen ledges. Excavations may be several feet deep.

Outdoor v. indoor hibernation

Natural hibernation offers some advantages, and some disadvantages. In its favour, freezing is very unlikely to occur – even under severe weather conditions – as at anything beyond a few inches underground temperatures are very stable indeed. Even in the most severe weather, frosts rarely penetrate more than 5cm (2in) deep. If your tortoise has safely hibernated itself in this way before, then there is no necessity to vary its

routine. Natural hibernation is not intrinsically dangerous. Be aware, however, that Mediterranean tortoises are especially susceptible to damp conditions, so any hibernation area must be very well drained or in a naturally dry habitat. The disadvantages of the method, however, include:

1 Flooding. If this should occur, then the tortoise is at serious risk.
2 Health inspections during hibernation are practically impossible.

Tips

- Do not allow tortoises to burrow in an area where flooding is possible.

- Perform extra-careful health checks throughout the summer and especially during the period immediately prior to hibernation.

- The area above a hibernating tortoise can be protected by covering the ground with wire mesh – but be watchful in warm weather as the tortoise may be trying to emerge!

3 There is always the danger of attack by foxes, raccoons (in the USA), rodents or similar predators (left).

Artificially controlled hibernation

In the majority of cases, we recommend that 'artificial' hibernation in a temperature-controlled environment is generally more satisfactory.

Some tortoises can prove difficult to 'settle' in hibernation, and may scrape the bottom out of cardboard boxes. A plywood box is recommended. This should be lined with thick polystyrene and shredded paper to provide a good layer of insulation. An inner box, containing the tortoise is then placed within this larger box. The entire container should then be placed in a dry, frost-free environment. Recently imported tortoises should not be hibernated unless they are in excellent condition. Suspect animals should be over-wintered in a warm, dry and well-ventilated terrarium. The most critical factor in hibernation is temperature stability. Maintaining the temperature within close parameters is absolutely critical to a successful and healthy hibernation.

Insulation merely slows down the rate of heat exchange; it does not prevent it altogether. Therefore, no matter how well you insulate, if you subject your tortoise's hibernation box to sub-zero temperatures for an extended period, it will still become too cold and the tortoise will die. If you allow your tortoise's hibernation box to get too warm for too long, it will begin to use up valuable fat and energy reserves and may even wake up too early. Generally, we recommend a maximum of four months

hibernation period – less for small specimens. The absolute critical minimum and maximum temperatures for a safe hibernation are:

Maximum = 10°C (50°F)
Minimum = 2°C (35°F)   *continued*

Below *Temperature stability is critical during hibernation. This system of two boxes provides an ideal environment.*

Insulation provided by a layer of polystyrene chips

Check temperatures regularly during hibernation. Be especially vigilant during severe cold spells.

Danger
- 12°C
- 10°C
Ideal
- 5°C
- 0°C
Danger

Above *Outdoor or natural hibernation allows the tortoise to excavate its own burrow instead of hibernating it in a box under controlled conditions.*

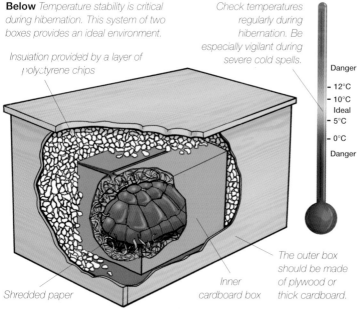

The outer box should be made of plywood or thick cardboard.

Inner cardboard box

Shredded paper

Above *Outside hibernation is usually safe because frost rarely penetrates very deep into the garden soil.*

Hibernation – outdoors or indoors

Under no circumstances whatsoever should a hibernating tortoise be subjected to prolonged exposure to temperatures higher than 10°C or lower than 2°C. Failure to appreciate the importance of this invariably leads to death or injury in hibernation. Blindness due to the eyes literally freezing solid is a particularly tragic consequence of allowing temperatures to fall too low.

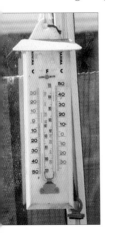

The easiest way to check temperatures is to obtain a maximum/minimum-reading greenhouse thermometer from any garden or hardware store. Check it at regular intervals, hourly if necessary in very cold spells. If sustained low or high temperatures are noted, temporarily move the tortoises into a more suitable place until temperatures stabilise to a satisfactory level again. Today electronic thermometers are available with built-in alarms that sound if the temperature goes outside pre-set limits.

Refrigerator hibernation

The ideal temperature for hibernation is 5°C or 40°F. At this temperature tortoises remain safely asleep, but are in no danger of freezing. In some areas, hibernation using a temperature-controlled refrigerator (not freezer) is recommended as a safe and reliable method of hibernating Mediterranean tortoises. However, if this method is used,

adequate air exchange is essential. Opening the door briefly once every 48 hours has proved successful. Each tortoise should be placed within the refrigerator in its own cardboard box. This box should be slightly larger than the tortoise, and should be partly filled with shredded paper. Place them in the refrigerator at a starting temperature of 12°C (54°F), and slowly reduce the temperature over the first week until it reaches a stable 5°C (40°F).

It should be noted that very small juveniles can be hibernated with perfect safety. They do so in the wild, and can also do so in captivity. However, temperature control and stability is critically important. We strongly recommend that the refrigerator method be used with tortoises under 76mm (3in) long. Greater temperature stability and safety can be assured by allowing the juveniles to bury into a tray containing a minimum 7.6cm (3in) depth of loose substrate comprised of fibrous potting compost, sand, and medium gravel. By surrounding themselves with this substrate, their effective mass is increased dramatically, improving thermal stability, and a more natural microclimate is also achieved, reducing the dangers of dehydration.

Protect from predators

If hibernating tortoises in a box in an attic, shed, outbuilding or similar location, be sure to monitor temperatures carefully, and

Tips

- Never attempt to hibernate any tortoise if you suspect it may be a tropical variety. Attempted hibernation of species that do not hibernate in nature is likely to lead to death.

- Do not attempt to feed a tortoise immediately prior to hibernation because if you hibernate it while the upper digestive tract contains food, it is in serious danger. Tortoises need a fasting period of at least three weeks at slightly lower than normal temperatures before hibernating.

- Remember that (in general) the smaller the tortoise, the more likely it is to end up as a hibernation casualty. Very small tortoises must be given a shorter, carefully controlled hibernation.

- Never attempt to hibernate a tortoise which you suspect is ill. To put a sick or underweight tortoise into hibernation is to condemn it to certain death.

Left *If you use cardboard boxes to hibernate your tortoises, take care to ensure that they are not vulnerable to attack by predators who could chew through the material.*

Below *A juvenile Hermann's tortoise. Most juveniles such as this can be safely hibernated for a period of between eight and 12 weeks, and can be woken up about a month before the adults would naturally wake.*

protect hibernation boxes from possible attack by rodents which are a serious hazard. A 'frost protection' heater may be required to ensure temperatures never approach freezing point. Please consult the Tortoise Trust's free guide *Safer Hibernation and Your Tortoise* for complete information on how to ensure hibernation success.

Waking up from hibernation

March to early April is the time when most adult tortoises will emerge naturally from hibernation. This is a critical time for them as they need to begin feeding as quickly as possible and can be vulnerable to illness and infection as their reserves are depleted. Check animals weekly through February and more frequently still through March, and be ready to remove them from hibernation if they are found to have woken, or have lost too much weight (any weight loss in excess of 10 per cent is cause for concern). Any that have urinated should be removed immediately. The following points should help owners to ascertain their pet's health status when they do wake.

Above *Check your tortoise's eyes when it wakes from hibernation – they should be clear and fully open.*

- The eyes should be open and bright. If not, bathe them in tepid water. If they still do not open properly, look for any signs of white matter or a cloudy haze on the cornea, or stickiness which could indicate an infection.

- Open the mouth and check the tongue colour. It should be a healthy pink, or orange-pink in North African tortoises.

Furthermore it should be free from white or yellow deposits. Check for an excessively red tongue which could indicate infection. If you have difficulty opening the mouth, watch carefully when the tortoise is put into water as the mouth should be seen to open very slightly when it drinks.

- After warming the tortoise up, and bathing it as described on page 38, it may be ready to eat, but some can take a few days. Others prefer to get straight on with eating and don't appear to need to drink.

Above *Check that the tongue is pink and healthy and free of deposits.*

Above *If necessary, clean the eyes, nose and mouth gently.*

Left *A basking lamp helps to warm up tortoises that are just out of hibernation.*

Right *To rehydrate the tortoise, soak it in a bowl filled with about 25mm (1in) of slightly warm water.*

However, continue to soak for ten minutes a day for a few days and watch out for the first passing of urine. This can often be somewhat thick or yellowish at first but the urates should return to the normal white within a few days.

• Check the tail for any unusual smells or exudations, especially yellowish substances. A slight infection inside the tail is not uncommon especially in active mating males. If found, however, it will need veterinary treatment.

• Be very aware of the status of any tortoises remaining in hibernation as time goes on. Check daily for movement and urination. By April, be ready to remove any that are still slumbering. Don't leave anything to chance.

• Don't forget that tortoises will not feed if their body temperature is not high enough. Provide a supplementary basking lamp in cool or dull weather. Tortoises must have extra heat and light at this sensitive time to get their bodies functioning properly.

Index

Page references in *italic* type refer to illustration captions

Photographic credits

Bigstockphoto.com: Steve McBill: 13 top. Paul van Eykelen: 14 top left. Werg: 53 top left.

Jane Burton, Warren Photographic: Front cover top left, front cover (egg), front cover centre, 2, 40 top right, 52 both centre, 60 left.

Crestock.com: Ameng Wu: 1, 3.

Dreamstime.com: Mikhail Blajenov: 49 bottom left. Eric Isselée: 59 top right. Jean Morrison: 32. Nico Smit: 8. Temelko Temelkov: 11 bottom right.

Fotolia.com: Besieteneuve: 20 bottom. Choucashoot: 7 top. Gabriel-Ciscardi: 37 bottom. Harmonie57: 33 centre. Ideen: 50. Eric Isselée: 5. Jesus: 36. Philippe Leridon: Back of jacket centre left. Lomskij: 38-39. Michael Luckett: 33 bottom right. Walter Luger: 61 top right. Matze: 7 centre. Thomas Mounsey: 27 (daffodil). Julija Sapic: 28.

Andrew and Nadine Highfield: 7 bottom, 9 centre, 9 bottom, 11 top left, 11 top right, 12, 13 bottom right, 15 top right, 15 bottom right, 16 bottom right, 17 centre right, 17 bottom, 19 top, 19 bottom, 21 top right, 21 bottom right, 22, 25 top, 26 both, 27 bottom left, 27 bottom right, 29 all three, 33 bottom right, 34, 35 bottom left, 35 bottom right, 37 centre right, 38 left, 39 top right, 39 bottom, 40 bottom right, 41 bottom left, 41 centre right, 43 top right, 43 bottom right, 44, 45 bottom left, 45 bottom right, 46, 47 centre left, 47 bottom

left, 47 bottom right, 48, 49 top right, 51 all three, 52 bottom, 53 bottom, 54, 55 centre right, 59 centre left, 59 bottom right, 60 top right, 61 centre right.

Interpet Archive: 23 (all images), 61 top left.

iStockphoto.com:
Selahattin Bayram: Front cover centre right. Maria Bibikova: 37 top right. Denice Breaux: 57 bottom right. Norman Chan: 40 centre (lettuce).
Michael Chen: Front cover bottom, 6-7, 20 left, 20-21, 21 left. Rachel Dunn: 41 top. Darren Gidney: 57 centre right. Tracy Hebden: 27 (anemone), 55 top right. Eric Isselée: 4, 47 top right, 58 top right. Silvia Jansen: Back of jacket top right (leaves). Stefan Klein: 43 (millipede). Oleg Kozlov: 56. Alexander Kuzolev: 43 (snail). Trevor Norman: 58 left. Uros Petrovic: 40 centre left. Jon Rasmussen: 27 (foxglove). Mehmet Salih: Back of jacket bottom. Igor Semenov: 43 bottom right. Cecilia Spitznas: 27 (hydrangea). Margo van Leeuwen: 27 (sweet pea). Michael Walker: 53 top right. Maria Zhuravleva: Back of jacket top right (flower).

Shutterstock Inc.:
George Nazmi Bebawi: 13 centre. Julie DeGuia: 6 top border (et seq.). Elpis Ioannidis: 39 top left. Eric Isselée: 11 centre, 16 centre, 16 centre right, 17 centre left, 18 top left, 24. Joseph Moore: 10-11. Sean Nel: 25 top centre. PhotoSky 4t com: 14-15. Urosr: 25 bottom. Werg: 13 bottom left.